Kwanzaa

By Trudi Strain Trueit

Reading Consultant
Cecilia Minden–Cupp, PhD
Former Director of the Language and Literacy Program
Harvard Graduate School of Education
Cambridge, Massachusetts

Children's Press®
A Division of Scholastic Inc.
New York Toronto London Auckland Sydney
Mexico City New Delhi Hong Kong
Danbury, Connecticut

Designer: Herman Adler
Photo Researcher: Caroline Anderson
The photo on the cover shows a family celebrating Kwanzaa.

Library of Congress Cataloging-in-Publication Data

Trueit, Trudi Strain.
  Kwanzaa / by Trudi Strain Trueit.
    p. cm. — (Rookie read-about holidays)
  ISBN-10: 0-531-12458-4 (lib. bdg.)   0-531-11839-8 (pbk.)
  ISBN-13: 978-0-531-12458-1 (lib. bdg.)   978-0-531-11839-9 (pbk.)
    Kwanzaa—Juvenile literature. 2. African Americans—Social life and
customs—Juvenile literature. I. Title. II. Series.
  GT4403.A2T78 2006
  394.2612—dc22   2006003958

CHILDREN'S PRESS, and ROOKIE READ-ABOUT®, and associated
logos are trademarks and/or registered trademarks of Scholastic Library
Publishing. SCHOLASTIC and associated logos are trademarks and/or
registered trademarks of Scholastic Inc.
1 2 3 4 5 6 7 8 9 10 R 16 15 14 13 12 11 10 09 08 07

Kwanzaa (KWAN-zah)
celebrates African American
culture and history.

Kwanzaa was created in 1966 by an African American teacher named Maulana Karenga (mah-LAH-nah kah-RING-ah).

Kwanzaa gets its name from an ancient harvest festival. The name means "first fruits" in Swahili (swah-HEE-lee). Swahili is an African language.

Maulana Karenga

December 2007

Sunday	Monday	Tuesday	Wednesday	Thursday	Friday	Saturday
						1
2	3	4	5	6	7	8
9	10	11	12	13	14	15
16	17	18	19	20	21	22
23	24	25	26	27	28	29
30	31					

6

Kwanzaa lasts from December 26th to January 1st.

January 2008						
Sunday	Monday	Tuesday	Wednesday	Thursday	Friday	Saturday
		1	2	3	4	5
6	7	8	9	10	11	12
13	14	15	16	17	18	19
20	21	22	23	24	25	26
27	28	29	30	31		

Kwanzaa has seven
principles to live by.
Each day of Kwanzaa focuses
on a different principle.
Day One: Unity
Day Two: Self-determination
Day Three: Collective work
                 and responsibility
Day Four: Cooperative
                 economics
Day Five: Purpose
Day Six: Creativity
Day Seven: Faith

Working together to build a home is an example of the principle of Day Three.

A Kwanzaa table

Families gather around a table every night during Kwanzaa. The table is decorated with fruits, vegetables, and other items.

Everyone drinks from one cup called a unity cup. Each person says the name of an important African American as the cup is passed.

The unity cup

A kinara

Someone lights a new candle in the kinara (kee-NAH-rah).

A kinara is a candleholder. It holds seven candles— one for each night of Kwanzaa. The candles are the African colors of black, red, and green.

Everyone talks about
the principle for that
night. They share ideas
on how to make it a part
of their life.

A Kwanzaa gathering

An elder leading a ceremony during Kwanzaa

African American families
gather for a big Kwanzaa
feast on December 31st.
They sing and dance.
People shout, "Harambee!"
(hah-RAHM-bay).
Harambee means
"Let's pull together!"

Ways to Celebrate

Most families decorate
for Kwanzaa. They hang
photos, artwork, and
banners. Some people put
up a Kwanzaa tree. It may
be a fir or palm tree.

A decorated home

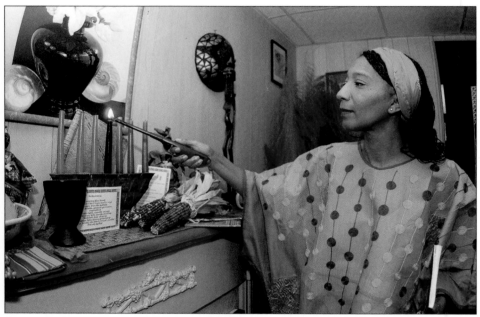

A woman wearing special African clothing

Many people dress in traditional African clothing during Kwanzaa. They wear red, black, and green, or other colorful fabrics.

People usually exchange
small gifts at Kwanzaa.
The gifts are called zawadi
(sah-WAH-dee).

Exchanging zawadi during Kwanzaa

Creating zawadi for a Kwanzaa festival

Many people give home-
made zawadi to honor the
sixth principle of creativity.
They create cards,
paintings, or bookmarks.

Children may give the gift of music. On the last night of Kwanzaa, they sing and play the songs they have written. It is an exciting celebration!

Boys playing traditional African drums

Words You Know

celebration

decorate

kinara

30

Maulana Karenga

unity cup

zawadi

31

Index

About the Author

Trudi Strain Trueit is a former television news reporter and weather forecaster. She has written more than thirty fiction and nonfiction books for children. Ms. Trueit lives near Seattle, Washington, with her husband Bill.

Photo Credits

Photographs © 2007: AP/Wide World Photos: 18 (Karin Cooper), 22 (Mark Moran/The Citizens Voice), 5, 31 top left (Ken Ruinard); Corbis Images/ Royalty-Free: 14, 30 bottom right; Getty Images: cover (Mark Adams), 3 (Tom Wilson); Photo Researchers, NY/Lawrence Migdale: 17, 30 top; PhotoEdit: 26 (Cindy Charles), 29 (Kayte M. Deioma), 21 (Patrick Olear), 9 (A. Ramey), 24, 31 bottom (David Young-Wolff); Superstock, Inc./Brand X: 13, 31 top right; The Image Works/Colette Fournier: 10, 30 bottom left.